Maximilian Kolbe

Saint for Anointing of the Sick

1894-1941

Born in Zdunska Wola, Poland

Feast Day: August 14

Patron saint of the 20th century, journalists, prisoners, people with drug problems, families, and the prolife movement

Text by Barbara Yoffie
Illustrated by Jeff Albrecht

Dedication

To my family:
my parents Jim and Peg,
my husband Bill,
our son Sam and daughter-in-law Erin,
and our precious grandchildren
Ben, Lucas, and Andrew

To all the children I have had the privilege of teaching throughout the years.

Imprimi Potest:
Stephen T. Rehrauer, CSsR, Provincial
Denver Province, the Redemptorists

Imprimatur:
In accordance with CIC 827, permission to publish has been granted on September 28, 2018, by the Most Reverend Mark S. Rivituso, Auxiliary Bishop, Archdiocese of St. Louis. Permission to publish is an indication that nothing contrary to Church teaching is contained in this work. It does not imply any endorsement of the opinions expressed in the publication; nor is any liability assumed by this permission.

Published by Liguori Publications, Liguori, Missouri 63057
To order, visit Liguori.org or call 800-325-9521.

ISBN 978-0-7648-2798-3

Liguori Publications, a nonprofit corporation, is an apostolate of the Redemptorists. To learn more about the Redemptorists, visit Redemptorists.com.

Printed in the United States of America
22 21 20 19 18 / 5 4 3 2 1
First Edition

Dear Parents and Teachers:

Saints and Me! is a series of children's books about saints, with six books apiece in the first four sets. The first set, *Saints of North America,* honors holy men and women who blessed and served the land we call home. The second, *Saints of Christmas*, includes heavenly heroes who inspire us through Advent and Christmas and teach us to love the Infant Jesus. The third, *Saints for Families*, introduces saints who modeled God's love within and for the domestic Church. The fourth, *Saints for Communities,* explores individuals from different times and places who served Jesus through their various roles and professions.

The seven books in the *Saints for Sacraments* series explore eight saints who had great love for the sacraments. John the Baptist baptized Jesus in the Jordan River. Padre Pio helped people make a good confession. Teresa of Ávila was known for her great love of the Eucharist. Philip Neri received the Holy Spirit after praying to God. Louis and Zélie Martin, a married couple, taught their children to serve God and the poor. At an early age, John Vianney wanted to dedicate his life to God as a priest; today he is the patron saint of parish priests. Maximilian Kolbe battled poor health to become a priest and brought God's healing to sick people.

Name the saint who lived in the desert and ate locusts and honey. In this set of books, who was the saint with stigmata? Who began a Carmelite convent dedicated to prayer? Who grew up during the French Revolution? Which saints were the parents of Thérèse of Lisieux? Who volunteered to die in place of a stranger in a prison camp? Find out in the *Saints for Sacraments* set—part of the *Saints and Me!* series—and help children connect to the lives of the saints.

Introduce your children or students to the *Saints and Me!* series as they:

—**READ** about the lives of the saints and are inspired by their stories.

—**PRAY** to the saints for their intercession.

—**CELEBRATE** the saints and relate them to their lives.

Saints for Sacraments

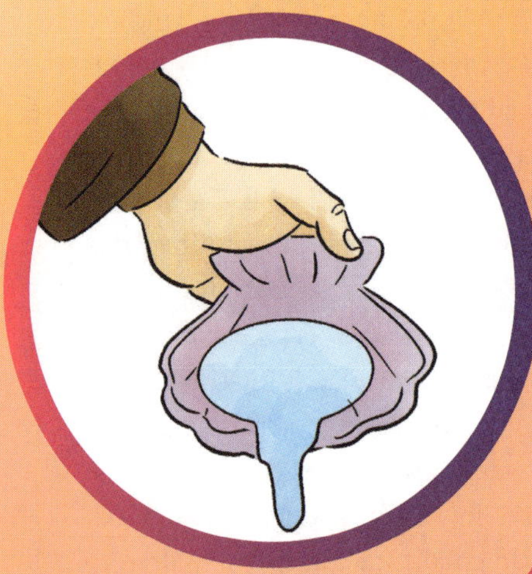

John the Baptist
Baptism

Teresa of Ávila
Eucharist

Philip Neri
Confirmation

Padre Pio
Reconciliation

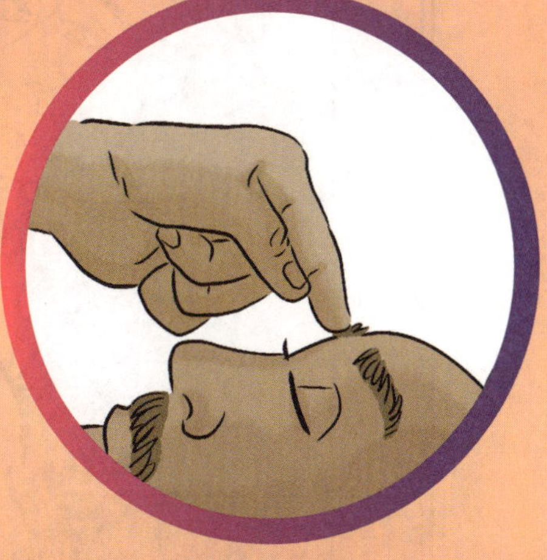

Maximilian Kolbe
Anointing of the Sick

Louis and Zélie Martin
Matrimony

John Vianney
Holy Orders

Maximilian Kolbe was a Polish Franciscan priest and missionary who loved God very much. He wanted people to know how much God loved them—in happy times and in sad times. God wants to give comfort to people who may be sick or suffering. He gives us the anointing of the sick, a sacrament of healing. This sacrament is a sign of God's love for us, especially when we suffer in our bodies or our minds. Maximilian Kolbe shared God's love with many people.

The Kolbes named their second baby boy Raymond. Raymond liked to play and have fun! He also liked to pray. His mother taught him how to pray the rosary. Raymond prayed the rosary every day. He loved Mary, the Mother of God, with all his heart.

When Raymond was young, Jesus' mother, Mary, appeared to him. He was so surprised! In her hands she held two crowns. One was white, and the other was red. "Which do you choose?" Mary asked him. The white crown meant he would serve God. The red crown meant he would become a martyr. Raymond smiled and said, "I will take both!"

Raymond entered the Franciscan seminary to study for the priesthood. He was a hard-working student and loved to learn new things. Raymond, now called Maximilian, was sent to Rome to finish his studies. During this time, he started a prayer group devoted to Mary. In 1918, he was ordained a Franciscan priest and returned to Poland to serve God's people.

Father Maximilian became very sick and went to the hospital to rest. He visited the other patients and told them, "I am praying for you. I hope you feel better soon." In the anointing of the sick, people receive the healing presence of Jesus. This sacrament gives people strength and courage to keep going even in sad times. The special prayers of the priest or bishop and the anointing with holy oil give the sick person peace and comfort.

Father Maximilian was a priest with many talents! He started the City of the Immaculate, a monastery and large center that printed Catholic magazines and newspapers. Later, he started a radio station! He used the gifts God gave him to teach people and spread the Catholic faith. "We must help people grow in their faith and teach them about Mary. Mary leads everyone to Jesus."

In 1930, Father Maximilian was sent to Japan as a missionary. He taught in the seminary. He started another monastery and a center for printing newspapers to teach about the faith. After six years, Father Maximilian returned to his monastery in Poland. He had lots of work to do!

World War II started in 1939. It was a terrible war. German soldiers came to Poland and arrested people. They put them in prison camps. Father Maximilian hid thousands of people in his monastery so they would not be arrested. "They have no home and nothing to eat. We can help them," he said.

Before long, Father Maximilian was arrested and taken to a big prison camp. It was a very sad place. All the prisoners wore striped uniforms. The guards were mean. They made the prisoners work extremely hard. Sometimes the prisoners did not have enough food to eat.

Father Maximilian shared his food with the other prisoners. He heard confessions and offered Mass in secret. He prayed with them and told them, "Don't ever forget to love." This was a hard lesson to learn in a prison camp. "Father Maximilian is very kind," said the prisoners.

Then one day, a prisoner escaped! Ten prisoners would be punished because the man ran away. One of them cried out, "My wife! My children!" Father Maximilian told the guard, "Take me instead." The guard shouted, "Who are you?" Father Maximilian replied, "I am a Catholic priest. That man has a wife and children. I want to take his place."

The ten prisoners were put in a small prison cell without food or water. God worked through Father Maximilian to give comfort, peace, and courage to the suffering prisoners. They sang songs to Mary and prayed together. Father Maximilian helped them to feel at peace. Sadly, after several days, all the men died. A guard said, "I have never seen anything like this before. That priest was a brave man."

The anointing of the sick is given to those who are very sick. Older adults may receive this sacrament, too! Like all the sacraments, the anointing of the sick gives special graces. These graces make us strong and brave like Father Maximilian. You will feel the peace and love of Jesus when you receive the anointing of the sick.

Father Maximilian loved people just like Jesus did. He celebrated the sacraments, shared his great love for Mary, and served the people of God. His newspapers and magazines spread the faith to millions of people. He is best known as the Catholic priest who gave his life for another man. In 1982, Pope John Paul II canonized Father Maximilian Kolbe, calling him a martyr of charity.

Love is a gift God gives you to share,
Reach out in love and show that you care.

Saint Maximilian Kolbe,
you loved Jesus
and his mother, Mary.
Your heart was full of love
for other people.
Help me share my love
and think of others
before myself.
Amen.

GLOSSARY (New Words)

Cell: A room where a prisoner is kept

City of the Immaculate: A monastery and large center with many buildings used for publishing Catholic reading materials

Grace: The gift of God's life in us

Holy oil: Oil of the sick, which is blessed by the bishop at the chrism Mass on Holy Thursday

Martyr: Someone who gives up his or her life for a belief or cause

Missionary: A person who teaches the faith or preaches the gospel in a certain place

Monastery: A place where priests and religious live

Ordained: To receive the sacrament of holy orders and become a deacon, priest, or bishop

Prison camp: A camp where prisoners of war are watched by guards

Sacrament: One of seven special signs of God's life and love

Seminary: A school where men are trained to be priests

World War II: Also called the Second World War, it was fought in Europe, Africa, and Asia from 1939–1945